THE DUTIES *of*
BROTHERHOOD
in ISLAM

Translated from the
Iḥyā' of Imām al-Ghazālī

MUHTAR HOLLAND

THE ISLAMIC FOUNDATION

THE ISLAMIC FOUNDATION, Markfield Conference Centre,
Ratby Lane, Markfield, Leicestershire, LE67 9SY, UK
Tel: 01530-244944/5, Fax: 01530-244946
E-mail: i.foundation@islamic-foundation.org.uk
http//www.islamic-foundation.org.uk

Quran House, P.O. Box 30611, Nairobi, Kenya

PMB 3196, Kano, Nigeria

. . . to my spiritual brothers and sisters

Contents

Foreword   7

Translator's Foreword   9

Introduction: The Time and Place of al-Ghazali   13

AL-GHAZALI: *On the Duties of Brotherhood*
The first duty: *material assistance*   21
The second duty: *personal aid*   30
The third duty: *holding one's tongue*   35
The fourth duty: *speaking out*   49
The fifth duty: *forgiveness*   60
The sixth duty: *prayer*   70
The seventh duty: *loyalty and sincerity*   72
The eighth duty: *informality*   78
Postscript   89

Translator's Notes   93

Foreword

Man is lonely today, as he never was.

You live in a crowded world; you are tied into an intricate network of social links and bonds; like a tiny atom, you are whirling around in the company of a multitude of others like you, acting and interacting with each other; yet, you are 'lonely'. 'Loneliness' is one of those 'gifts' which modern secularist and technological civilisation has bestowed upon you. For your bonds, however numerous, have been drained of warmth; your links, however sophisticated, have turned mechanical; the entire network of your social relationships has become an abstract mosaic, devoid of life and intensity. And with what consequences – alienation, personality disturbance, emotional distress, a high crime rate and empty lives.

Unless the human bonds are again infused with affection and the warmth of love and brotherhood, man will never be able to taste the rich joys and pleasures of living together. It is this blessing of love and brotherhood which is one of the greatest sources of sustenance and nourishment for man – spiritually, morally, intellectually, socially and even physically. The 'lonely' man – a product of our age – is wandering in search of bonds which will not snap like dry twigs and leave him in the lurch.

One of the greatest blessings of Islam is its admirable success in creating strong, warm, rich and durable bonds of love and brotherhood between man and man. It has done so on the basis of faith in one God, *tawḥīd;* but it has also inspired man to follow a pattern of behaviour which will sustain and strengthen mutual brotherhood. The book now before you, *Duties of Brotherhood in Islam*, attempts to present those very norms and values of conduct which make brotherhood in Islam so enduring and so affectionate.

I am grateful to my colleague, Brother Muhtar Holland, for having rendered into English this enormously useful portion of Al-Ghazali's monumental *Iḥyā' 'Ulūm al-Dīn* Al-Ghazali needs no introduction and his name is itself a sufficient guarantee of the charm and effectiveness of the treatment of such an important subject in this book. But I must add that Brother Muhtar has done a very commendable job in preserving and transmitting the original charm in a new vehicle of communication.

The book was originally published in 1975 by Latimer New Dimensions Ltd., London, and, as it happened, was instrumental in establishing our association with Brother Muhtar. I am very grateful to him for having allowed us to bring out this second impression.

I have every hope that the book will be welcomed by both Muslims and non-Muslims alike. Muslims will be able to use it as a mirror and teacher – to learn, to correct and to strengthen what they still retain of that powerful brotherhood. Non-Muslims should be able to catch a glimpse or two of the rich treasure of divine guidance which was finally given to the Prophet Muhammad fourteen hundred years ago, and which inheritance they share with us.

In conclusion I pray to Allah to bless our efforts with His acceptance and mercy.

4 February 1980   **KHURRAM J. MURAD**
16 Rabi' al Awwal 1400   Director General

Translator's Foreword

Bismillāhi'rraḥmāni'rraḥīm

'In the Name of the One God, All-Merciful,
All-Loving!'

The conditions of life on this planet permit no man or woman to be 'an Iland, intire of it selfe.' If this was ever less than obvious, it has become self-evident in an age when the home of mankind is appropriately described as 'Spaceship Earth'.

Outwardly at least, we all find ourselves involved, willy-nilly, in a whole network of relationships with other people. But what of the quality of these relationships? Do they not often seem impersonal and superficial? For all our multifarious involvements and commitments, chosen or forced upon us, do not many of us feel *inwardly* isolated from other human beings?

Many wonders there be, said the ancient Greek poet, but naught so strange as man. There may be some in our midst with such great confidence in themselves, such vast inner resources, that they feel no need of fellowship in any form. There may be some whose faith in Almighty God is so great and so constant that mere human company is insignificant to them. I suspect the membership of either group to be very small indeed. I confess that I belong to neither – much as I may envy the former, and admire the latter.

Through the vicissitudes of my own outer life, I have tried, I suppose, to achieve a reasonable measure of self-sufficiency and a reasonably balanced adjustment to the rest of the world. I have had my share of frustrations and failures, and any success I have known can be ascribed only in part to my own efforts. But it is rather of my inner life that I wish to speak – presuming that it might hold some interest for the reader of a work on brotherhood!

I believe that from an early age I have been aware – only obscurely, maybe – of the difference between two worlds. One is a world outside myself, in which I have made certain movements, or lived a certain kind of life; the other is somehow within me, an inner world in which I have also moved and lived. There have been times, no doubt, when I was so immersed in the activities of the outer of these worlds that I became virtually unconscious of the inner. There have been other times when the world within has been a haven of retreat from the apparent incoherence of the one outside. There have even been rare occasions when the two worlds met, when life moved freely and harmoniously between them both.

From my own taste of it, I would say that the most complete experience of freedom and harmony, of being at one with oneself and with the whole world, must be seen as something 'given', as a grace or blessing from God Almighty. This is beyond any ordinary comprehension. On a less exalted plane, I have found, in one way or another throughout my life, that fellowship with other human beings is the most effective way of avoiding isolation in my own, imperfect, inner world. I have long been seeking after what seems the ideal situation: to live and work in the outer world together with others of like mind and heart and with common spiritual aspirations.

When I came to feel the need to espouse a religion (meaning to commit myself to one 'for better or worse', as opposed to flirting with religiousness on the one hand, or to nominal membership from birth on the other), it was Islam that I chose to embrace. As for adopting a particular religion, I had come to the conclusion – after many misgivings – that this was an important part of the fulness of human experience. As for the choice of Islam, one consideration was the directness and blazing simplicity of its doctrine: I could see truth in other religions, but here the Truth was plainest *to me*. The second consideration was the Islamic emphasis on brotherhood.

I had been stirred by the Qur'anic ideal of a brotherhood of believers 'in the Way of God'; I had been moved literally to tears by accounts of the fraternal acts of the Prophet Muhammad and his Companions (what openness in the feelings they must have known); I was also influenced by my personal encounters with Muslims of today. I had met Muslims from all walks of life, in my travels in Turkey and Syria, and during a five-month study-leave in Egypt. I had lectured to students from all parts of the Muslim world: Nigeria, Egypt, Sudan, Syria, Iran, Pakistan, Malaysia, Bahrain, even Mecca itself. Now Muslims themselves would be the last to pretend that the Islamic world today embodies more than a fraction of the true religious ideal. Nevertheless, I sensed that, among very many of the Muslims I came to know, the spirit of brotherhood was very much alive and expressed itself in their attitudes and behaviour.

When I discovered al-Ghazali's writing on the Duties of brotherhood and fellowship it was my own interest, in the first place, that impelled me to make an English translation. The act of translating from the Arabic was a strong experience for me, at once helpful and painful. It was helpful in that I found, while working, that many things became clear to me concerning my relationships with other people. It was also painful in that I was made acutely aware of many shortcomings in my attitudes and behaviour towards those whose brother I sought to be, and indeed towards my fellow human beings in general.

Having found that my translation was well received by my most intimate friends, I eventually felt the wish to share it more widely. The author of the original work was, of course, a Muslim – writing for Muslims nearly nine hundred years ago. The translator is also a Muslim. I certainly hope that this translation will be read by fellow Muslims (there may well be far more who know English than can read classical Arabic). I am sure we can all profit from sitting awhile together at the feet of al-Ghazali. I ask to be forgiven if I have failed in what I intended: to let al-Ghazali speak in an alien tongue, without distorting his meaning, to an age not his own.

It is also my sincere hope that this work will be read by many who are not Muslims. As sons and daughters of Adam and Eve, we are all brothers and sisters. We all yearn for an improvement in the quality of our human relationships, and I believe that al-Ghazali has helpful suggestions for us all, regardless of our religious allegiance. We are all fellow-passengers aboard Spaceship Earth – need our inner worlds be so far apart?

Introduction

THE TIME AND PLACE OF AL-GHAZALI

The Western reader is likely to have been taught a version of world history centred upon Europe – probably upon the British Isles in particular, if he or she is of the English-speaking peoples. If we wish to transport ourselves, by an act of the imagination, into the era in which al-Ghazali lived, it may help if we take as the key to our time-machine that most familiar of all dates, 1066 and all that. When 'all that'– the Battle of Hastings and the Norman Conquest of England – was happening, al-Ghazali was a small boy. By the Christian chronology he was born in 1058 and lived till the year 1111. It was during that span that the First Crusade was launched, the city of Jerusalem falling to the Crusaders in 1099.

The First Crusade produced a spectacular meeting between the Christian West and the Islamic East. It was to the latter that al-Ghazali belonged. His full name was Abu Hamid Muhammad ibn Muhammad al-Tusi al-Shafi'i al-Ghazali[1]: 'al-Tusi' indicating that his birthplace was Tus, a town in that part of the world nowadays called Persia or, more properly, Iran.

While it is convenient to contrast the 'Christian West' with the 'Islamic East', we need to recall that at this period the domains of Islam extended not only into Central Asia and India, but also across North Africa and into Spain. It was during al-Ghazali's lifetime that

Sicily was lost to the Normans, but despite a success at Toledo in 1085 the Christians were still centuries away from the final reconquest of Spain. We must also remember that Eastern Christendom still held sway in Byzantium, and would keep Constantinople almost as long as the Muslims clung to Granada.

Most of the vast territories of Islam had been won by the Arabs within a hundred years of the death, in 632, of the Prophet Muhammad (may God bless him and give him Peace!). Under the unifying rule of the Caliphs, ruling in the name of Allah, the One Almighty God, and following the path of His Messenger, a great civilisation developed. The Arabs made a contribution of fundamental importance – the Arabic language; but Muslims (and indeed also non-Muslims) of many races contributed to this civilisation. Those of Persian descent were prominent in the heyday of the Abbasid Caliphate of Baghdad. By the time of al-Ghazali, Turks had begun to play a leading role. In fact the Caliph had become a figurehead – symbolically of great importance still, though without the substance of power – and his 'protection' had fallen, just at the time of al-Ghazali's birth, to the Seljuq Turks. By the Islamic reckoning, it was in the year 450 that al-Ghazali was born.

The Seljuqs became the standard-bearers of Islam in the fight against Byzantium and against the Western Crusaders. They decisively routed the former at Manzikert in 1071, but failed, as we have seen, to hold Jerusalem from the latter in 1099. This failure was due in part to the fact that the Seljuqs were weakened by their efforts in another struggle. As well as defending Islam against the infidel from without, they were upholding 'orthodox' or 'mainstream' Islam in the face

14

of powerful and dangerous schismatics: the Fatimids of Egypt, and the notorious Assassins[2] of Alamut. It is this second, internal, struggle which is more important in its bearing on the career of al-Ghazali.

The main body of the Islamic community believed that its leaders were the successors, Caliphs, to the temporal authority of the Prophet. Not having inherited his spiritual powers, their duty was to act as guardians of the community against external foes and to govern that community in accordance with the Sacred Law as known from God's Word in the Qur'an and from the Sunna, the example set by God's Messenger (on him be Peace!). There were groups or movements, however, whose members believed that leadership rightly belonged to descendents of the Prophet through his son-in-law Ali and daughter Fatima. Those of this persuasion are known in general as the Shi'a, though they appear under many particular names. It was as the Fatimids that they seized control of Egypt nearly a century before the birth of al-Ghazali. The Shi'a saw in their leader something far more autocratic than a custodian of the Law who was himself governed by it. For them, the leader was himself the Law, since he was in receipt of infallible divine guidance. Their doctrines undermined the whole traditional basis of the main Islamic community.

In order to spread their doctrines, the Fatimid Shi'a attached what one might call a jesuitical importance to education. They established in Cairo, in conjunction with al-Azhar mosque, an institution which is said to be the world's oldest university.[3] In response to this challenge, the Seljuqs initiated an ambitious educational programme of their own and a vizier called

Nizam al-Mulk founded colleges in the major cities of the Seljuq domain. At one of these institutions al-Ghazali became a student, and at another he was appointed professor. At Nishapur he proved a brilliant scholar in law[4] and theology and he was still in his early thirties when he became principal teacher at Nizam's college in the capital city of Baghdad. His lectures attracted a large following. As a powerful weapon in the ideological warfare with the Fatimids, he enjoyed the favour of the highest circles.

Crusaders and Fatimids were not the only enemies of traditional Islam. Another threat came from the philosophers. There was a danger that rationalising tendencies might lead the intelligentsia to put reason above the belief in divine revelation on which the community was founded. Al-Ghazali made a profound private study of philosophy, and he delivered a fatal blow to its practitioners in a work called *The Incoherence of the Philosophers*.[5]

For all his glittering success, al-Ghazali was inwardly dissatisfied. Despite his remarkable intellectual achievements, the Truth eluded him and he could find no peace at heart. His spiritual crisis caused physical symptoms which actually interfered with his lecturing. On the pretext of making the Pilgrimage to Mecca, he left Baghdad behind. He had resolved to abandon his career for the life of hardship, abstinence and devotional worship.

It seems that in his early life al-Ghazali must have had some contact with the strand in traditional Islamic life that is generally known as *taṣawwuf* – the way of the Sufi. This he was now to try for himself, having failed to quench his thirst at the wells of law, theology and

16

philosophy. His wanderings took him not only to Mecca, but also to Damascus, Jerusalem (a few years before its capture by the Crusaders), and Hebron. Eventually he returned to a quiet life with a community of disciples in his native town of Tus. For a few years he was prevailed upon to give public lectures again in Nishapur, then he returned to Tus to die. The year of his death was 505 of the Islamic era.

THE ACHIEVEMENT OF AL-GHAZALI

Muslims believe that a Renewer of the Faith appears at the beginning of each century. What experience had happened to, or within, al-Ghazali after he left Baghdad? Because as a result of that experience he came to be seen as the Renewer for the sixth Islamic century. Indeed, he came to be known as *Ḥujjat al-Islām* or 'The Proof of Islam'.

It seems pointless to speculate about the exact nature of the experience which transformed al-Ghazali, and brought him the peace he had missed. We know from his own account that the Truth – always beyond even his formidable powers of systematic reasoning – came to him at last as something received rather than acquired. It came as a 'flash of light' sent by God into 'that secret thing which is sometimes expressed by spirit, and sometimes by soul'.

Once an inner certainty had made him spiritually whole, al-Ghazali was able to use his outstanding faculties and vast learning to integrate and revitalise the whole Islamic tradition. Through his direct personal

17

contacts, and through his many writings, he showed how every element in that tradition could and should be turned to its true purpose. That purpose was to help the believer to live a life devoted to the service of the One Almighty God, in constant remembrance of Him, and in preparation for the Life Hereafter.

Reason could lead men astray into trusting only the cleverness of their own minds. But al-Ghazali showed that in its right place, firmly subordinated to God's revealed guidance, it could be a useful instrument of clarification. The ascetic, devotional and mystic practices of the Sufi way could result in unbalanced excesses. But al-Ghazali showed how they could, if not divorced from normal observance of religious duties and ethics, open up a whole dimension of inner understanding.

It is certain that al-Ghazali made an incalculable and enduring contribution to the development of Islamic religion and society. Consider his influence in the important sphere of education. According to a recent writer, 'After al-Ghazali . . . the character of Muslim education, in aims, content, methods and institutions was determined for centuries. It hardly changed till the last hundred and fifty years.'[6]

Professor W. Montgomery Watt goes so far as to say: 'Al-Ghazali has been acclaimed by both Muslim and European scholars as the greatest Muslim after Muhammad.'[7]

AL-GHAZALI'S WRITINGS

Like most Muslims of his time, al-Ghazali wrote mainly in classical Arabic, though some of his books were written in the Persian language. This does not seem to be the place for a catalogue of his very considerable literary output, but it is necessary to say something about his major work. His great opus (four large tomes in Arabic) is entitled *Iḥyā' 'ulūm al-dīn*, which may be translated as 'The Quickening of Religious Knowledge', or 'The Revival of the Religious Sciences'. It is in this work that al-Ghazali deals with every aspect of the outer and inner life of the Muslim. The first quarter covers the Islamic forms of worship: ritual prayers, fasting, pilgrimage and so on. The second quarter considers the behaviour of the Muslim as member of a community of believers. The third treats of the perils of the soul. The fourth is devoted to the means of salvation.

ON THE DUTIES OF BROTHERHOOD

The treatise here presented in English translation comes from the second quarter of the *Iḥyā'*.[8] Brotherhood is a relationship of fundamental importance in Islam. The whole Community of Believers is conceived of as a great Brotherhood. 'Surely the believers are but brothers. So set things right between your two brothers, and be aware of God – perhaps you will obtain mercy.' (*Qur'ān 49.10*). More specifically, it has been the custom since the earliest times – following the example of the Prophet himself (God bless him and give him Peace!) – for Muslims to commit themselves to a 'contract' of brotherhood with fellow Muslims. Al-Ghazali shows how brotherhood can be an aid to spiritual purification and the perfection of one's worship, as well as a source of help and comfort in this world.

In the following pages the reader will encounter al-Ghazali's vast erudition in Qur'an and Prophetic Tradition, his familiarity with the insights of saints and mystics, his acceptance of the enlightening stories of the Jews and Christians, his skill as a jurist in disentangling a knotty point of law, his elevating theology, his psychological understanding, his logical acuity. Above all, I believe the reader will meet in al-Ghazali the wise elder brother – and the faithful servant of the One Almighty God.

AL-GHAZALI
On the Duties of Brotherhood

KNOW that the contract of brotherhood is a bond between two persons, like the contract of marriage between two spouses. For just as marriage gives rise to certain duties which must be fulfilled when it is entered into,[9] so does the contract of brotherhood confer upon your brother a certain right touching your property, your person, your tongue and your heart – by way of forgiveness, prayer, sincerity, loyalty, relief and considerateness.

In all, this comprises eight duties:

1

The first duty is the material one.
God's Messenger (God bless him and give him Peace!) said:

> – Two brothers are likened to a pair of hands, one of which washes the other.

He chose the simile of the two hands, rather than the hand and the foot, because the pair are of mutual assistance towards a single aim. So it is with two brothers; their brotherhood is only complete when they are comrades in a single enterprise. In a sense the two are like one person. This entails a common participation in good fortune and bad, a partnership in the future as in the present moment, an abandonment of possessiveness and selfishness. In thus sharing one's property with one's brother there are three degrees.

The lowest degree is where you place your brother on the same footing as your slave or your servant, attending to his need from your surplus. Some need befalls him when you have more than you require to satisfy your own, so you give spontaneously, not obliging him to ask. To oblige him to ask is the ultimate shortcoming in brotherly duty.

At the second degree you place your brother on the same footing as yourself. You are content to have him as partner in your property and to treat him like yourself, to the point of letting him share it equally. Al-Hasan said there was once a man who would split his waist-band between himself and his brother.

At the third degree, the highest of all, you prefer your brother to yourself and set his need before your own. This is the degree of the *ṣiddīq*,[10] and the final stage for those united in spiritual love.

Self-sacrifice is one of the fruits of this degree. Tradition tells how a Sufi fraternity were slanderously misrepresented to one of the Caliphs, who ordered their execution. Now one of their number was Abu'l-Husayn al-Nuri, who ran forward to the executioner so that he might be the first to be put to death. Asked why, he replied:

– I wished that my brothers rather than I
should have that moment to live.

22

This, to cut a long story short, was the cause all of their lives being saved.

If you do not find yourself at any of these stages in relation to your brother, then you must realise that the contract of brotherhood is not yet concluded in the Inner. All that lies between you is a formal connexion, lacking real force in reason or religion.

Maymun ibn Mahran said:

> – One who is content not to put his brother first might as well be brother to the People of the Tombs!

As for the lowest degree, this is also unacceptable to truly religious people. Tradition tells that 'Utba al-Ghulam came to the house of a man whose brother he had become, saying:

> – I need four thousand of your money.

The other said:

> – Take two thousand.

'Utba declined the offer, saying:

> – You have preferred this world to God. Are you not ashamed to claim brotherhood in God when you can say such a thing?

You ought to avoid worldly dealings with one at the lowest stage of brotherhood. Abu Hazim said:

> – If you have a spiritual brother do not deal with him in your worldly affairs.

By this he meant 'if he is at this stage'.

As for the highest degree, this corresponds to the description of the true believers given by God (Exalted is He!) when He said:

> – They agree their affairs by mutual consultation, and spend freely of what We have bestowed upon them. (*Qur'ān 42.38*)

That is, they are co-owners of worldly goods without distinctions of status. There were those who would shun the fellowship of a man who used the expression '*my* shoe', thereby attributing it to himself.

Fath al-Mawsili once came to a brother's house while he was away. Telling his brother's wife to bring out his chest, he opened it and took from it what he needed. When the slave-girl later informed her master he exclaimed:

> – If what you say is true, you are a free woman for the sake of God!

So delighted was he at his brother's deed.

Once a man approached Abu Hurayra (may God be pleased with him!) and said:

> – I wish to take you as my brother in God.
> – Do you know what brotherhood entails?
> – No.
> – That you have no greater right to your pounds or your pence than I have.
> – I have not yet reached that stage.
> – Then begone from me!

'Ali son of al-Husayn (may God be pleased with both!) said to a man:

> – Does one of you put his hand in the pocket or purse of his brother and take what he needs without permission?
> – No.
> – Then you are not brothers!

Some people called upon al-Hasan (may God be pleased with him!) and asked:

> – Abu Sa'id, have you done your (*ṣalāt*) prayer?[11]
> – Yes.

24

– Because the market folk have not yet prayed.

– And who takes his religion from the market folk?

I hear that one of them would refuse his brother a penny. Al-Hasan said this as if it amazed him.

A man came to Ibrahim ibn Adham (may God be pleased with him!) as the latter was leaving for Jerusalem, and said:

– I wish to be your travelling-companion.

– On condition that I have more right to your goods than you yourself.

– No.

– I admire your sincerity!

Now this Ibrahim ibn Adham (may God be pleased with him!) would never differ with a man who accompanied him on a journey, and he would only choose for a companion someone who was in harmony with him. His fellow on one occasion was a sandal-thong merchant. At a certain staging-post someone presented Ibrahim with a bowl of broth. He opened his companion's bag, took a bundle of thongs, set them in the bowl and returned it to the giver of the present. When his companion came along he asked:

– Where are the thongs?

– That broth I ate, what did it cost?

– You must have given him two or three thongs.

– Be generous and generosity will be shown you!

He once gave a donkey belonging to his companion, without his permission, to a man he saw walking. When his companion came along he said nothing and did not disapprove.

'Umar's son (may God be pleased with them both!) said that one of the companions of God's Messenger (God bless him and give him Peace!) was given a sheep's head. He said:

> – My brother so-and-so needs it more than I do,

and sent it to him. That person sent it on to another. Thus it was passed from one to another till it came round again to the first, after being through seven hands.

Tradition tells that Masruq owed a heavy debt. His brother Khaythama was also in debt, so Masruq went and paid off Khaythama's debt without his knowledge, and Khaythama went and paid off Masruq's debt without *his* knowledge.

When God's Messenger (God bless him and give him Peace!) witnessed the brotherhood between 'Abd al-Rahman ibn 'Awf and Sa'd ibn al-Rabi', the latter offered to put the former first both materially and spiritually. 'Abd al-Rahman said:

> – God bless you in both respects,

thus preferring his brother in the same way as his brother preferred him. It was as if he accepted then returned the compliment. This is equalising, whereas the first gesture was preferment. Preferment is worthier than equalising.

Abu Sulayman al-Darani used to say:

> – If I owned the whole world to put in the mouth of a brother of mine I would still deem it too little for him.

He also said:

– I feed a morsel to a brother of mine and find the taste of it in my own throat.

Spending on brothers is even worthier than giving alms to the poor, for ʿAli (may God be pleased with him!) said:

– Twenty dirhams I give to my brother in God are dearer to me than one hundred I give in alms to the needy.

He also said:

– To make a meal and gather my brothers in God around it is dearer to me than to free a slave.

In putting others first, all follow the example of God's Messenger (God bless him and give him Peace!). He once entered a thicket with one of his companions and gathered two toothpicks, one of them crooked and the other straight. The straight one he gave to his companion, who said:

– O Messenger of God, you are more entitled to the straight one than I!

But he replied:

– When a comrade accompanies a comrade, if only for one hour of the day, he will be asked to account for his companionship, whether he fulfilled his duty to God therein or whether he neglected it.

He indicated by his own example that putting the companion first is to fulfil one's duty to God in fellowship.

On another occasion God's Messenger (God bless him and give him Peace!) went out to a well to wash at it. Hudhayfa ibn al-Yaman took a robe and stood screening God's Messenger while he washed. Then

Hudhayfa sat down to wash himself, and God's Messenger (God bless him and give him Peace!) took his turn to stand screening Hudhayfa from view with the robe. But he objected saying:

> – My father be your ransom, and my mother too! O Messenger of God, do not do it!

Yet he (God bless him and give him Peace!) insisted on holding the robe as a screen while Hudhayfa washed, and he said:

> – Each time two people are in company together, the dearer to God is he who is kinder to his companion.

Tradition tells that Malik ibn Dinar and Muhammad ibn Wasi' went together to the house of al-Hasan while he was out. Muhammad ibn Wasi' took out a basket of food from under al-Hasan's bed and began to eat. Malik said to him:

> – Clap your hands to fetch the master of the house.

But Muhammad paid no attention to his words and went on eating, for Malik was more for politeness and manners than he. Then al-Hasan arrived and said:

> – My dear Malik, we were not used to being so shy one of another till you and your fellows appeared.

With this he indicated that to make oneself at home in one's brothers' homes is part of true brotherhood. And indeed, God (Exalted is He!) said:

> – Or of your friend, or to which you have the keys. (*Qur'ān 24.61*)[12]

For although one brother would give the keys of his house to another, permitting him to act as he saw fit, a brother felt that piety required him to refrain from eating, until God (Exalted is He!) revealed this Verse and allowed them to help themselves to the food of brothers and friends.

2

The second duty is to render personal aid in the satisfaction of needs, attending to them without waiting to be asked, and giving them priority over private needs.

Here too there are different degrees, as in the case of material support.

The lowest degree consists in attending to the need when asked and when in plenty, though with joy and cheerfulness, showing pleasure and gratitude.

Someone said:

> – If you ask your brother to satisfy a need, and he does not do so, then remind him, for he may have forgotten. If he still does not do it, pronounce '*Allāhu akbar!*' over him and recite this Verse: 'As for the dead, God will raise them up.' (*Qur'ān 6.36*)[13]

Ibn Shubruma once satisfied a great need for one of his brothers, who later brought him a present.

> – What is this? asked Ibn Shubruma.
> – For the favour you did me.
> – Keep it and may God preserve you! If you ask your brother for something you need and he does not exert himself to satisfy your need, then wash for prayers, pronounce four

takbir[14] over him and count him among the dead.

Ja'far ibn Muhammad said:

> – I make haste to satisfy the needs of my enemies, lest I reject them and they do without me.

If this be the attitude towards enemies, how then towards friends?

A Muslim in the early days would see to the maintenance of his brother's wife and children for forty years after his brother's death, attending to their needs, visiting them daily, and providing for them from his wealth so that they missed only the father's person; indeed they were treated as not even by their father in his lifetime. It was known for a man to go regularly to the door of his brother's household and enquire:

> – Have you oil? Have you salt? Is there anything you need?

If anything was needed he would attend to it unbeknown to his brother.

This is how brotherhood and compassion are shown. If a man does not manifest compassion towards his brother in the same degree as to himself, then there is no goodness in it.

Maymun ibn Mahran said:

> – If you reap no benefit from a man's friendship his enmity will not hurt you.

God's Messenger (God bless him and give him Peace!) said:

> – Surely God has vessels on His earth, namely our hearts. And the vessels dearest to God (Exalted is He!) are the purest and strongest

and finest: purest from sins, strongest in the Faith, finest towards their brothers.

In short, your brother's need ought to be like your own, or even more important than your own. You should be on the watch for times of need, not neglecting his situation any more than you would your own. You should see that he does not have to ask, nor to reveal his need to appeal for help. Rather should you attend to it as if you did not know that you had done so. You should not see yourself as having earned any right by virtue of what you have done, but rather count it a blessing that he accepts your effort on his behalf and your attention to his affair. You should not confine yourself to satisfying his need, but try from the start to be even more generous, to prefer him and put him before relatives and children.

Al-Hasan used to say:
> – Our brothers are dearer to us than our families and our children, because our families remind us of this world while our brothers remind us of the Other.

Al-Hasan also said:
> – If a man stands by his brother to the end, then on the Day of Resurrection God will send angels from beneath His Throne to escort him to the Garden of Paradise.

Tradition tells that whenever a man visits a brother, longing to meet him, an angel calls out from behind him:
> – You have done well, and it shall be well for you in the Garden of Paradise!

'Atā'said:
> – Seek out your brothers after three occasions.

If they are sick, visit them, If they are busy, help them. If they have forgotten, remind them.

It is related that Ibn 'Umar was looking about to right and left in the presence of God's Messenger (God bless him and give him Peace!), who asked the reason. He replied:

– There is someone dear to me and I am searching for him, but do not see him.

– If you love someone, ask his name, his father's name, and where he lives, then if he is sick, visit him and if he is busy, help him.

(Another version adds the words, '. . . and the name of his grandfather and that of his tribe.')

Al-Sha'bi said of a man who keeps the company of another, then says he knows his face but not his name:

– That is the knowledge of fools.

Ibn Abbas was asked:

– Who is the dearest of men to you?

– One who sits in my company, he replied.

He also said:

– If someone sits in my company three times without having need of me, I learn where he is placed in the world.

Sa'id ibn al-'Ās said:

– I owe my sitting-companion three things: on his approach I greet him; on his arrival I make him welcome; when he sits I make him comfortable.

God (Exalted is He!) said:

– Full of mercy one to another. (*Qur'ān 48.29*)[15]

These words point to compassion and generous treatment.

Part of complete compassion is not to partake in solitude of delicious food, nor to enjoy alone an occasion of happiness; rather should the brother's absence be distressing and the separation sad.

3

The third duty concerns the tongue, which should sometimes be silent and at other times speak out.

As for *silence*, the tongue should not mention a brother's faults in his absence or his presence. Rather should you feign ignorance. You should not contradict him when he talks, nor dispute nor argue with him. You should not pry and quiz him about his affairs. On seeing him in the street or about some business, you should not start a conversation about the object of your coming and going, nor ask him about his, for perhaps it will be troublesome to him to discuss it, or he may have to lie about it.

Keep silent also about the secrets he confides in you, and on no account divulge them to a third party – not even to his closest friends. Do not reveal anything about them, not even after separation and estrangement, for to do so would be meanness of character and impurity of the Inner.

Keep silent from criticism of his dear ones, his family and his children; also from relating other people's criticism of him, for it is your informant who directly abuses you.

Anas said that God's Messenger (God bless him and give him Peace!) never faced anyone with something displeasing to him, for the hurt comes immediately from the informant and only indirectly from the original speaker.

Of course you should not hide any praise you may hear, for the pleasure in it is received directly from the conveyer of the compliment as well as indirectly from the original source. Concealment here would mean envy.

In short, you should keep silent about any speech unpleasant to him in general and in particular – unless obliged to speak out to promote good and prevent evil,[16] and even then only if you can find no valid excuse for saying nothing. In such cases you need not worry about his disapproval, since what you do is beneficial to him when rightly understood, even if it looks bad at first sight.

As for mentioning his misdeeds and faults, and the misdeeds of his family, this is slander and unlawful in respect of every Muslim. Two things should turn you from it.

First examine your own condition and if you find there one blameworthy thing then be tolerant of what you see in your brother. It may be that he is unable to control himself in that particular characteristic, just as you are impotent in the face of your own difficulty. So do not be too heavy on him on account of one blameworthy trait – what man is completely upright? Wherever you find yourself lacking in your duty to God, do not expect as much from your brother in his duty to you, for your right over him is not greater than God's right over you.

Second, you know that were you to seek for someone free of all blemish you would exhaust the entire

Creation without ever finding a companion. For there is not one human being who does not have both good qualities and bad, and if the good outweigh the bad that is the most that can be hoped for.

The noble believer always keeps present in himself the good qualities of his brother, so that his heart may be the source of honour, affection and respect. As for the hypocrite of low character, he is always noticing misdeeds and faults.

Ibn al-Mubarak said:

> – The believer tries to find excuses for others, while the hypocrite looks out for mistakes.

Al-Fudayl said:

> – Manliness is pardoning the slips of one's brothers.

This is why the Prophet (God bless him and give him Peace!) said:

> – Seek refuge with God from the bad neighbour who sees some good and conceals it, sees some bad and reveals it

There is no-one at all whose condition cannot be improved in some respects, or made worse.

Tradition tells how a certain man praised another in the presence of God's Messenger (God bless him and give him Peace!) then blamed him the very next day. So he (Peace upon him!) said:

> – You praise him one day and blame him the next!
>
> – Yesterday I told the truth about him, and today I did not lie about him. He pleased me yesterday so I told the best I knew of him. He angered me today so I spoke the worst I knew of him.

To this he (God bless him and give him Peace!) said:

> – Reasoned argument can be sorcery.

He evidently disapproved of it, since he likened it to sorcery. Thus he said, in another traditional report:

> – Abuse and argumentation are twin branches of hypocrisy.

And further:

> – God disapproves of argumentation for you: all argumentation.

Al-Shafi'i (may God have mercy on him!) said:

> – There is not one Muslim who obeys God without ever transgressing against Him, nor is there one who transgresses against Him without ever obeying Him. If a man's obedience outweighs his transgressions, then he is righteous.

If such a man be accounted righteous in his duty to God, how much more should you consider him righteous in his duty to you and the obligation of your brotherhood.

Just as it is incumbent upon you to hold your tongue from mentioning his misdeeds, so ought you to observe silence in your heart. This is done by giving up suspicions, for suspicions constitute slander in the heart, which is also unlawful. Keep within the bounds by not putting a bad construction on his action, so long as you can see it in a good light. As for what is revealed unmistakably and before your very eyes, so that it is impossible for you not to know about it, you should if possible ascribe what you witness to absent-mindedness and forgetfulness.

Suspicion is formed in two ways; first, by what is

called perception, which rests on some outward sign. This causes a necessary movement of the thinking which cannot be set aside. Secondly, there is that which arises from your prejudice against someone. There emanates from him some act which could be taken in either of two ways; but your prejudice against him causes you to settle for the worse interpretation, even though there is no outward sign to justify it. This is an offence against him in the Inner, something unlawful in respect of every believer. For the Prophet (God bless him and give him Peace!) said:

> – God has forbidden one believer to tamper with the blood, property or honour of another, or to hold a bad suspicion of him.

Also:

> – Beware of suspicion, for suspicion is the most untruthful report, and suspicion leads to prying and spying.

Further:

> – Do not spy and do not pry. Do not sever relationships and do not fall out, but serve God as brothers.

Prying consists in listening to rumours, spying in visual observation.

Concealing faults, feigning ignorance of them and overlooking them – this is the mark of religious people. You have sufficient notice of the perfect degree in concealing what is ugly and revealing what is good, in that God (Exalted is He!) is so qualified in the prayer where it is said:

> – O Thou Who revealest the beautiful and concealest the ugly!

What is desirable in God's sight is that we model

our character after His, for He is the Veiler of faults, Forgiver of sins, Indulgent towards His creatures. So how can you fail to be indulgent towards one who is your equal or your superior, but in no way your slave or your creature?

Jesus (Peace be upon him!) said to the Disciples:

> – How do you act when you see a brother sleeping, and the wind blows off his clothes?
> – We screen him and cover him.
> – Rather do you lay bare his private parts.
> – Glory be to God! Who would do such a thing?
> – One of you listens to gossip about his brother, then adds to it and passes it on exaggerated.

You must know that a man's belief is incomplete so long as he does not wish for his brother what he wishes for himself. The lowest degree in brotherhood is where you treat your brother as you would wish to be treated yourself, and there is no doubt that he would expect you to veil his shame and keep quiet about his misdeeds and faults. If shown the opposite of what he expected he would be very annoyed and angry. How unworthy then, if he were to expect what he himself would not conceive and intend. Woe to him then in the words of the Book of God (Exalted is He!), for He says:

> – Woe to the givers of short measure, who exact in full when others measure out to them, but skimp in measuring or weighing out to others! (*Qur'ān 83.1–3*)

All who demand fair treatment beyond what they themselves dispense come under the import of this Verse.

The source of deficiency in veiling another's shame, and of striving to display it, is a hidden disease of the Inner, namely rancour and envy. For the rancorous and envious has his Inner full of dirt, but keeps it imprisoned in his Inner, conceals it and does not show it as long as he lacks a pretext. But when he finds an opportunity the restraint is released, the reserve is abandoned, and the Inner sweats with its hidden dirt.

Whenever the Inner is wrapped up with rancour and envy it is better to break off relations. Some wise men say that open blame is better than hidden rancour. The only thing to soften the rancorous is isolation. If a man carries in his heart a bad feeling towards another Muslim, then his belief is weak, his affair is risky, and his heart is dirty and unfit to meet God.

'Abd al-Rahman ibn Jubayr ibn Nafir reported that his father told him:

> – When I was in the Yemen I had a Jewish neighbour who used to tell me about the Torah. This Jew came to me after a journey, and I said to him, 'God has sent a Prophet amongst us, who has summoned us to Islam, and we have submitted. He has also revealed to us a Book, which confirms the Torah.' The Jew said, 'You speak the truth, yet you cannot carry out what he has brought you. We find his description and that of his community in the Torah; he does not allow a man to cross the doorstep with hatred in his heart for his Muslim brother.'

Part of the matter is keeping quiet, and not divulging a brother's secret which he has entrusted to you. You should deny knowledge of it, even if this means

41

lying, for to speak the truth is not incumbent in every circumstance. Just as it is permitted to a man to hide his own faults and secrets, even if he needs to lie, so may he do for his brother's sake. For his brother stands in his own shoes and the pair are like one person, different only in body. This is the true nature of brotherhood.

Furthermore, in what one does in one's brother's presence one should not be hypocritical, nor abandon one's private for one's public behaviour. For your brother's knowledge of what you do is like your own knowledge of it, without distinction.

The Prophet (may God bless him and give him Peace!) said:

> – If a man veils his brother's shame, God will veil him in this world and the Other.

Or in another report:

> – . . . it is as if he restores to life a baby girl buried alive.[17]

He (God bless him and give him Peace!) also said:

> – If a man gives information, then looks about him, it is a confidence.

And:

> – All sessions are confidential bar three: that in which blood is shed unlawfully, that in which unlawful sexual intercourse takes place, and that in which property is unlawfully used.

And again:

> – When two sit down in session together their proceedings are confidential, and neither of them may divulge anything distasteful to the other.

A man of culture was asked:

42

– How do you keep a secret?

– I am its tomb!

There is a saying:

– The breasts of free men are the tombs of secrets.

According to another:

– The fool's heart is in his mouth, but the intelligent man's tongue is in his heart.

That is, the fool cannot conceal what is inside him, but unconsciously blurts it out. Therefore it is necessary to break off relations with fools and to beware of their company, nay the very sight of them.

Another was asked:

– How do you keep a secret?

– I deny knowledge of the informant and give my oath to the questioner.

Yet another said:

– I hide it, and hide the fact that I am hiding it.

Ibn al-Muʿtazz expressed himself in verse:

– Entrusted with a secret, I undertake to hide it.
So I bank it in my breast, and that becomes a
    vault for it.

Another poet, wanting to develop the theme, said:

– The secret in my breast is not like the inmate
    of a tomb;
For I see that one entombed expects the
    Resurrection.
. I prefer to forget it until it might seem
That I never had of it the least recollection.
Could the secret between us be hidden away,
From the heart and the bowels it would never
    see day.

Someone disclosed a secret of his to his brother.
He asked him later:

> – Have you remembered it?
>
> – No, I have forgotten it!

Abu Sa'id al-Thawri used to say:

> – If you wish to take a man as your brother,
> anger him then contrive to bring him in
> contact with somebody who will ask him about
> you and your secrets. If he speaks well of you
> and hides your secret, then make him your
> fellow.

Abu Yazid was asked:

> – Whom would you take as your fellow?
>
> – One who knows of you as much as God
> knows, then hides it as God hides it.

Dhu'l-Nun said:

> – There is no good in the fellowship of one who
> only likes to see you immaculate.

One who divulges a secret when angry is of base
character, for all sound natures demand that it be
hidden when one is content. A wise man said:

> – Do not take as your fellow one whom you
> find changeable under four conditions: when
> he is angry or content, when he is greedy
> or desirous.

Rather should true brotherhood be firm against any
change in these conditions. Thus it is said:

> – See how the noble, when you sever your
>   bond,
> Still hides the bad and plays you true.
> See how the vile, though you stick to your
>   bond,
> Still hides the fine and plays you false.

Al-'Abbas said to his son 'Abdullah:

> – I see this man (meaning Umar, may God be pleased with him!) preferring you over the elders. So remember five bits of advice from me: on no account divulge a secret to him; on no account slander anyone in his presence, on no account give currency to a lie about him; on no account disobey him in anything; on no account let him catch you in any treachery.

Al-Sha'bi said:

> – Every word of these five is better than a thousand.

Silence includes abstaining from contention and contradiction whatever your brother talks about.

Ibn Abbas said:

> – Do not dispute with the fool, for he will hurt you; nor with the mild man, for he will dislike you.

The Prophet (God bless him and give him Peace!) said:

> – If a man gives up contention when he is in the wrong, a house will be built for him within the Garden of Paradise; but if a man gives up contention even when he is in the right, a house will be built for him in the loftiest part of the Garden.

While it is his duty to give it up if he is in the wrong, the reward for what is above duty is made greater. For to remain silent when one is right is harder on the soul than keeping quiet when one is wrong. Recompense is in proportion to the effort.

The most serious causes that fan the fire of rancour between brothers are contention and disputation. These are the very essence of variance and rupture. For rupture starts off with opinions, then becomes verbal and finally physical.

The Prophet (Peace be upon him!) said:

> – Do not fall out one with another, do not hate one another, do not envy one another, do not break off one with another. Serve God as brothers, The Muslim is brother to the Muslim. He does not wrong him or offend him or forsake him. A man can do no worse than disgrace his Muslim brother.

The worst disgrace is contention, for if you reject what another says you accuse him of ignorance and stupidity, or of forgetfulness and absent-mindedness in understanding his subject. All this constitutes disgrace, annoyance and alienation.

According to the tradition of Abu Umama al-Bahili:

> – God's Messenger (God bless him and give him Peace!) came out to us as we were disputing. He was angry and said, 'Give up contention because there is little good in it. Give up contention because the use of it is small, and it stirs up enmity among brothers.'

One of the early believers said:

> – If a man quarrels and disputes with his brother his manliness diminishes and his virtue goes.

'Abullah ibn al-Hasan said:

> – Beware of disputing with men, for you will never negate the cunning of the mild nor the onslaught of the vile.

One of the early believers said:
- The most impotent of men is he who falls short in seeking brothers, yet even more impotent is he who loses those he has won. Much contention causes loss and estrangement, and bequeaths enmity.

Al-Hasan said:
- Do not buy the enmity of one man for the love of a thousand men.

In general the only motive for contention is to display intellectual superiority and to belittle one's opponent by showing up his ignorance. This amounts to arrogance, contempt, hurtfulness, and the insulting charge of folly and ignorance. There is no meaning to enmity but this, so what part can it have in brotherhood and true friendship?

Ibn 'Abbas reported the Messenger of God (God bless him and give him Peace!) as saying:
- Do not dispute with your brother, do not mock him, and do not go back on your promise to him.

He (God bless him and give him Peace!) also said:
- You will not win people with your wealth. What will win them is a cheerful face and a good character.

Contention is incompatible with such goodness of character. The early believers went to great lengths in guarding against contention, and in urging mutual assistance; so much so that they frowned on questioning altogether. They said:
- If you say to your brother 'Come along!', and he asks 'Where?', then do not make him your fellow.

47

According to them he should rather come along unquestioningly.

Abu Sulayman al-Darani said:

> – I once had a brother in Iraq. I would go to him when times were bad and say, 'Give me some of your money.' He would throw me his purse for me to take what I wanted. Then one day I came to him and said, 'I need something.' He asked, 'How much do you want?' And so the sweetness of brotherhood left my heart.

Another said:

> – If you ask your brother for money and he says, 'What are you going to do with it?' he has abandoned the duty of brotherhood.

Know that the mainstay of brotherhood is concord in word and deed, and compassion. Abu 'Uthman al-Hiri said:

> – Concurring with brothers is better than having compassion for them.

And it is as he said.

4

The fourth duty is to use the tongue for speaking out.

Just as brotherhood calls for silence about unpleasant things, so it requires the utterance of favourable things. Indeed, this is more particularly a feature of brotherhood, because anyone satisfied with silence alone might as well seek the fellowship of the People of the Tombs. You wish for brothers so as to benefit by them, not just to escape being hurt by them, and the point of silence is to avoid hurt.

You should use the tongue to express affection to your brother, and to enquire agreeably about his circumstances. For instance, in asking about some accident that has befallen him, you should show the heart's concern on his behalf and over his slow recovery. Thus you should indicate by word and deed that you disapprove of all circumstances that are disagreeable to him, and use your tongue to let him know that you share his joy in all conditions that give him pleasure. For brotherhood means participating together in joy and sadness.

The Prophet (God bless him and give him Peace!) said:

> – If one of you loves his brother, let him know it!

He gave this command because the communication brings about an increase in love. If the brother knows that you love him he will naturally love you, without a doubt. If you know that he loves you too, then without a doubt your love will increase. Thus love will grow progressively from either side and will multiply.

Mutual love among believers is required by the Sacred Law, and is desired in religion. Therefore the Messenger pointed out the way of it, saying:

> – Guide one another, love one another.

Part of the matter is calling your brother by his favourite names, be he absent or present. Umar (may God be pleased with him!) said;

> – There are three ways of showing sincere brotherly love: give him the greeting 'Peace!' when first you meet him, make him comfortable, and call him by his favourite names.

Another part is praising him for the good qualities you know him to possess, in the presence of one before whom he would choose to be praised. This is one of the most efficacious ways of attracting affection. Likewise praising his children, his family, his skill and his actions; then on to his intelligence, his character, his appearance, his handwriting, his poetry, his composition, and everything he enjoys. All this without lying or exaggeration, though it is necessary to embellish whatever admits of embellishment.

Still more fundamental is that you communicate to him the praise of anyone who praises him, showing your pleasure, for to hide such praise would be pure envy.

Furthermore, you should thank him for what he

does on your behalf, indeed for his very intention even if he does not succeed completely. 'Ali (may God be pleased with him!) said:

> – He who does not praise his brother for his good intention will not praise him for his good deed.

What is even more potent in attracting affection is defending him in his absence whenever he is abused or his honour impugned, explicitly or by innuendo. Brotherhood calls for briskness in protection and aid, for rebuking the fault-finder and addressing him harshly. Not to speak out here disturbs the breast and alienates the heart. It is a shortcoming in fulfilling the duty of brotherhood. When the Messenger of God (God bless him and give him Peace!) compared two brothers to a pair of hands, one of which washes the other, he meant that one should aid the other and stand in for him.

God's Messenger (God bless him and give him Peace!) said:

> – The Muslim is brother to the Muslim. He does not wrong him, does not forsake him, does not betray him.

What treachery and desertion to abandon him to the rending of his honour! It is like abandoning him to the rending of his flesh. How vile in a brother to see you savaged by a dog, tearing your flesh, yet remain silent and unmoved by compassion and zeal to defend you! The rending of honour is harder on souls than the rending of flesh, which is why God (Exalted is He!) compared it with the eating of carrion meat. For He said:

> – Would any of you like to eat the flesh of his brother's corpse? (*Qur'ān 49.12*)

The angel, who in dreams provides sensory representation of what the spirit has learned from the Preserved Tablet, symbolises slander by the eating of carrion. Thus if someone dreams he is eating carrion-flesh this means he is slandering people. For in his symbolism, that angel has regard for the correspondence and correlation between the thing and its symbol, the meaning of the symbol being understood spiritually and not in the outer forms.

Therefore, the protection of brotherhood by repelling the blame of enemies and the criticism of fault-finders is a duty in the contract of brotherhood.

Mujahid said:

– Refer to your brother in his absence only as you would have him refer to you in your absence.

There are two measures you can apply.

In the first case, when something is said about your brother, you consider what you would want him to reply on your behalf, if the same were said of you in his presence; then you must deal accordingly with the impugner of his honour.

In the second case, you suppose that he is present behind a wall, listening to your words, but thinking that you are unaware of his presence. Ask yourself how your heart would be moved to help him when you were in his hearing and sight, for so it should be in his absence.

Someone said:

– Whenever a brother of mine is mentioned in his absence I imagine him sitting there, and I say of him what he would wish to hear if he were present.

Another:

> – Whenever a brother of mine is mentioned
> to me I imagine myself in his form, then I say
> about him what I would wish said about me.

This is part of genuine Islam; that you do not see
fit for your brother what you do not see fit for yourself.

Abu'l-Darda' once watched a pair of bulls plough-
ing in a double-yoke. One of them halted to rub its
body and the other halted too. He wept and said:

> – So it is with two brothers working together
> for God. If one of them halts the other follows
> suit.

Through concord, sincerity comes to completion;
and he who is not sincere in his brotherhood is a hypocrite. Sincerity means equality between absence and
presence, between the tongue and the heart, between the
private and the public. Separateness, contradiction and
non-conformity in any of this is adulteration of true
affection. This is an infection of religion and an intrusion
on the way of the believers. So one who lacks the capacity in himself would do better to cut himself off and
retire, rather than seek brotherhood and fellowship;
for the duty of fellowship is onerous, not to be borne
except by one of true worth, and its reward is indeed
generous, not to be won except by the truly fit.

The Prophet (God bless him and give him Peace!)
said:

> – Abu Hirr! Be a good neighbour to your
> neighbour and you will be a Muslim. Be a good
> fellow to your companion and you will be a
> *Mu'min*.[18]

Observe how he makes *Imān* the reward for fellowship, and *Islām* the reward for neighbourliness. Thus

the distinction between the excellence of *Imān* and the excellence of *Islām* is defined as the distinction between the difficulty of fulfilling one's duty as a neighbour and that of fulfilling one's duty in fellowship. Fellowship gives rise to many duties in circumstances that follow one another in close succession, while neighbourliness gives rise to pressing duties only at wide intervals and not on a lasting basis.

This duty to use the tongue also embraces instruction and advice. For your brother's need of knowledge is no less than his need of money. If you are rich in knowledge you are obliged to share your abundance with him, and to instruct him in all that is useful to him in religious and worldly matters. If you teach and instruct him and yet he does not act in accordance with the knowledge you convey, then you are obliged to advise. This you do by pointing out the disadvantages of what he is doing and the benefits to be had by giving it up, by threatening him with what is distasteful to him in this world and the Other in order to deter him, by drawing attention to his shortcomings, by disapproval of what is ugly in his sight and approval of what is fine.

However, all this must be confidential so that no-one else knows about it. When it takes place in public it is reproof and ignominy, whereas in confidence it is compassion and advice.

The Prophet (God bless him and give him Peace!) said:

– The believer is a mirror to the believer.

By this he meant that one can see from the other what he cannot see from himself. Thus a man can profit from his brother by learning his own faults, whereas if left to himself he would lose this advantage, just as he can benefit from an ordinary mirror by becoming aware of the faults in his outward appearance.

Al-Shafi'i (may God be pleased with him!) said:

– To admonish your brother in private is to advise him and improve him. But to admonish him publicly is to disgrace and shame him.

Mus'ir was asked:

– Would you like to be informed of your faults?

– If the advice were confidential, yes. But not in the public forum.

He spoke truly, for advice before the crowd is ignominy. On the Day of Resurrection God (Exalted is He!) will remonstrate with the believer under His Wing, in the shadow of His Veil, acquainting him with his sins privately. The book of his deeds will be handed under seal to the angels, who will escort him to the Garden of Paradise. When they near the gate of the Garden they will give him the book, still sealed, for him to read.

As for those who are full of hate, they will be summoned before throngs of witnesses and their limbs will be required to speak of their shameful acts, so that their disgrace and ignominy will be increased. We seek refuge with God from disgrace on the day of the Greatest Review!

The distinction between rebuke and advice, then, is a matter of secrecy or publicity, just as the distinction between courtesy and hypocrisy depends on the purpose motivating your connivance. If you connive for the integrity of your religion and because you see it as conducive to your brother's good, then you are courteous. But if you connive for your own comfort, the

55

satisfaction of your desires, and the integrity of your influence in the world, in that case you are a hypocrite.

Dhu'l-Nun said:

> – In fellowship with God, only concord. In fellowship with men, only sincere advice. With the self, only opposition. With Satan, only enmity.

You may say: 'If advice includes mentioning faults, then it includes alienation of the heart, and how can that come into the duty of brotherhood?' So you must realise that alienation only results from mentioning a fault already known to your brother, while drawing his attention to what he is unaware of is compassion itself. It is encouragement for hearts; I mean the hearts of the intelligent, for it does not touch the hearts of fools.

Someone who draws your attention to a blameworthy action you are addicted to, or a blameworthy feature of your character, so that you can cleanse yourself of it, is like one who warns you of a snake or scorpion under your robe – he has shown concern lest you perish, and if you disapprove of that how great is your folly! Blameful characteristics are scorpions and snakes. They are deadly perils in the Other Life, for they sting hearts and spirits and the pain they cause is worse than external physical stings. They are created of God's kindled Fire.

Therefore 'Umar (may God be pleased with him!) used to seek such guidance from his brothers, with the prayer:

> – God have mercy on a man who shows his brother his faults!

Thus 'Umar asked of Salman when he came to him:

– What have you heard about me that you disapprove of? Tell me, so that I may try and put it right.

Since he insisted, Salman said:

– I have heard that you keep two sets of clothing, one to wear by day and the other by night. I have also heard that you combine two meals at one table.

Said ʿUmar (may God be pleased with him!):

– Of these two I have had enough. Have you heard anything else?

– No!

Hudhayfa al-Marʿashi wrote to Yusuf ibn Asbat:

– I hear that you traded your religion for two grams. You stopped by a milkman and asked, 'How much is this?' He replied. 'One sixth,' but you said, 'No, one eighth.' 'It is yours!' said he. Now that man knew you. Uncover your head of the veil of the negligent, and beware of the sleep of the dead! Know that a man who reads the Qur'an and is not satisfied, but chooses this world, is surely one of those who mock God's Signs. God (Exalted is He!) has characterised the liars by their hatred of advisers, for He said, 'But you do not love advisers.' (*Qur'ān 7.79*)

All this applies to a fault he is unaware of. When you know that he knows it himself, and is merely under a compulsion from his nature, then you ought not to unveil it if he conceals it. However, if he lets it be seen you must advise him kindly, now by hints, now explicitly, though not to the point of alienating him. If you know that advice will not avail, and that he is

57

compelled by his nature to persist, then it is better to say nothing at all about it. So much for what concerns your brother's interest in religion and in the world.

When it is a matter of a shortcoming in his duty towards you, what is required of you is patience, forgiveness, pardon, and turning a blind eye. To interfere in this case has nothing to do with advice at all.

Nevertheless, if the case is such that his persistence in his fault would lead to rupture, then remonstrating in private is better than rupture, allusion is better than the direct approach, correspondence is better than verbal address. Yet patience is best of all, since your object where your brother is concerned should be to correct yourself by having consideration for him, fulfilling your duty towards him, and bearing his deficiency patiently – not merely to enjoy his help and fellowship.

Abu Bakr al-Kattani said:

– A certain man kept me company and he was heavy on my heart, so one day I made him a present in the hope of relieving my heart; but to no avail. So one day I led him by the hand into the house, and said, 'Put your foot on my cheek!' He refused, but I insisted, 'You must!' Then he did it, and the thing left my heart.

Abu 'Ali al-Ribati said:

– I was companion to 'Abdullah al-Razi as he was going into the desert. He said, 'Either you or I must act as leader.' So I said, 'Rather you.' 'Then you must obey,' said he. 'Very well,' I agreed. Then he took a bag, filled it with provisions, and carried it on his back. When I said, 'Hand it to me!' he replied, 'Did you not say, "You are the leader"? Well then, you must obey.' That night we were caught by the rain. He stood at my head till morning, shielding me from the rain with a cloak he wore, while I sat there, saying to myself, 'If only I had died, sooner than said, "You be leader"!'

5

The fifth duty is forgiveness of mistakes and failings.

The failing of a friend must be one of two kinds; either in his religion, through the commission of an offence; or in his duty to you, through an omission in brotherhood.

In the case of religion, where he commits an offence and persists in it, you must advise him kindly so as to supply his deficiency, put his affairs in order, and restore him to a correct and virtuous state.

If you are incapable of this and he remains obstinate – at this point there is a divergence in the ways followed by the Companions and Successors of the Prophet, whether to maintain his right to affection or to cut off relations.

Abu Dharr (may God be pleased with him!) favoured severance. He said:

– If your brother turns his back on his duty, hate him as you used to love him.

He considered this the course dictated by love for God's sake and hate for God's sake.

As for Abu'l-Darda' and one group of the Companions, they took the opposite view. Abu'l-Darda' said:

– If your brother alters and changed his hue

do not desert him on that account, for your brother will sometimes be crooked and sometimes straight.

Ibrahim al-Nakha'i said:

– Do not break off from your brother and do not shun him on account of a sin he has committed, for he may commit it today but give it up tomorrow.

He also said:

– Do not tell people of the mistake of a learned man, for the learned may make a mistake and then leave it.

According to the tradition:

– Beware of the mistake of the learned. Do not cut him off, but await his return.

It is related about 'Umar that he once enquired after a man he had taken as a brother, and who had gone away to Syria. He asked someone who came to him:

– What has my brother been doing?

– That man is Satan's brother.

– Eh?

– He has committed the major sins, even lapsing into wine-drinking.

Telling his informant to let him know when he intended to return, 'Umar wrote to his brother:

– In the name of God All-Merciful. *Ḥā' Mīm*.[19] The revelation of the Book is from God, Almighty, All-Knowing, Forgiver of sins, Accepter of repentance, Stern in punishment . . . (*Qur'ān 40.1–3*)

He remonstrated with him under this quotation, and chided him. His brother wept when he read the letter, saying:

– God speaks true, and ʿUmar advises me truly.
So he repented and came back.

There is a story of two brothers, one of whom was smitten with a desire. He revealed it to his brother and said:

> – I have a blemish, so if you wish you may consider yourself released from your contract of brotherhood with me.

But the other said:

> – I am not one to dissolve our contract on account of your error.

Then he made a compact between him and God that he would neither eat nor drink till God cured his brother of his passion. For forty days he kept asking him about his desire. His brother kept saying that his heart was set in its condition, so he wasted away of sorrow and hunger. At the end of forty days the passion left his brother's heart, and he gave him the news. At last he ate and drank, having all but perished from emaciation and suffering.

It is related in the stories of the People of Israel that two godly brothers were upon a mountain. One of them came down to the town to buy a pennyworth of meat. He saw a harlot at the butcher's shop, gazed upon her, fell in love with her, and carried her off to a private place to copulate with her. After spending three nights with her, he was ashamed to return to his brother in view of his offence.

Meanwhile, his brother missed him and felt concern about him. He descended to the town and kept on asking about him till he was directed to him. Then he went in and found him sitting with the girl. He embraced him and began kissing him and hugging him, but the other denied all knowledge of him, being so ashamed. Then he said:

> – Come my brother, for I know your condition and your story, yet you were never better loved nor dearer to me than at this moment.

Now when he realised that what had happened had not lowered him in his brother's eye he arose and went away with him.

This reflects one school of thought, which is subtler and more penetrating than that of Abu Dharr (may God be pleased with him!), though his is more proper and safer.

You may well ask how I can call the other view subtler and more penetrating. You might argue that it is not permissible to initiate a contract of brotherhood with one who commits this offence, and that the contract would have to be dissolved; for when a legal relation holds good in the presence of an effective cause, analogy dictates that it must dissolve when the latter dissolves. In the case of brotherhood, the effective cause is mutual assistance in religion, which does not survive the commission of the offence.

When I speak of the subtler view, I refer to the way in which tenderness, consolation and benevolence are effective in recalling and inspiring repentance. For the sense of shame endures with continuing fellowship, whereas when relations are severed and his appetite cut off from fellowship he will be obstinate and persist in his ways.

When I speak of its being more penetrating, I mean that brotherhood is a contract on the same footing as kinship; once it is contracted the duty is confirmed, and that which the contract entails must be

63

fulfilled. Fulfilment includes not neglecting the days of his need and poverty – and poverty in religion is more acute than material poverty. He has been afflicted by calamity and harmed by adversity, in consequence of which he is impoverished in his religion. Therefore he must be watched and cared for, not neglected. No, he needs constant kindness to be helped to salvation from the disaster which has befallen him. Brotherhood is provision for the vicissitudes and accidents of time, and this is the hardest of misfortunes. Further, if the man of bad morals enjoys the fellowship of the godfearing, and observes his fear and his constancy, he will soon come back to righteousness and be ashamed to persist. Indeed, a lazy man in fellowship with an industrious one will be shamed by him into industry.

Ja'far ibn Sulayman said:

> – Whenever I flagged in my labours I would look at Muhammad ibn Wasi', and his attitude to obedience, so that my energy in worship returned to me, laziness departed from me, and I could work for a week.

This is the proof: fellowship is a bond of flesh, like the bond of blood-kinship, and it is not permissible to shun a kinsman on account of his offence. Thus God (Exalted is He!) said to His Prophet (may God bless him and give him Peace!), concerning his kinsfolk:

> – If they disobey you, say, 'I am quit of what you do.' (*Qur'ān 26.216*)

He did not tell him to say, 'I am quit *of you*,' having regard for the duty of kinship and the bond of blood-relationship.

To this Abu'l-Darda' referred when he was asked:

– Do you not hate your brother when he has
done such and such?

and he replied:

– I only hate what he has done, otherwise he
is my brother.

Brotherhood in religion is firmer than brotherhood
in kinship. A wise man was asked:

– Which is dearer to you, your brother or your
fellow?

– I only love my brother if he is a fellow to
me.

Al-Hasan used to say:

– How many a brother was not born of your
mother!

Therefore is it said that kinship needs affection,
but affection has no need of kinship. Ja'far al-Sadiq
(may God be pleased with him!) said:

– The affection of a day is a link. That of a
month is kinship. That of a year is a blood-tie.
If anyone cuts it, God will cut him off.

Thus fulfilment of the contract of brotherhood is
obligatory, once it has been concluded. This is our
response to the question about initiating brotherhood
with the immoral, for he has no prior right. If he does
have a prior connexion through kinship it is certainly
not proper to break with him; one should rather try
and improve him.

The evidence for our view is that it is neither
blameworthy nor reprehensible to avoid initiating
brotherhood and fellowship; indeed some authorities
hold that it is preferable to go one's own way. But as for
interrupting the continuance of brotherhood, this is
forbidden and intrinsically blameworthy. It stands in

65

relation to initial avoidance like divorce to the avoidance of marriage, divorce being more hateful to God (Exalted is He!) than avoidance of marriage. The Prophet (God bless him and give him Peace!) said:

> – The worst of God's creatures are those who spread slander, separating dear ones.

One of the early believers said, of hiding the mistakes of brothers:

> – Satan likes to cast this kind of thing upon your brother, so that you will shun him and break with him. How careful you must be of what is dear to your Enemy!

This is because causing separation between loved ones is one of the things dear to Satan, just as the commission of sin is dear to him. If Satan gains one of his objects, the second should not be added unto him! The Prophet (God bless him and give him Peace!) alluded to this when a man maligned another, who had committed an abomination, for he checked him, saying:

> – Whoa! Do not be Satan's aide against your brother!

All this makes clear the distinction between continuation and initiation, for mixing with the immoral is to be avoided, and so is separation from dear ones and brethren to be avoided. One who is free from having to keep in step with another is not like one who is not free; and initially he is free. We have seen that to avoid contact and to keep one's distance is preferable. About continuing what has been entered into there is some disagreement, so to fulfil the duty of brotherhood is the better course.

All that has been said above relates to errors in the

brother's religion. As for his error in brotherly duty, by which he causes alienation, there is no disagreement on the proper course being forgiveness and patience. Indeed, whenever a good interpretation is possible, or an excuse – whether obvious or far-fetched – can be advanced, this is obligatory in the duty of brotherhood.

It has been said that you should seek seventy excuses for your brother's misdeed, and if your heart will accept none of them you should turn the blame upon yourself, saying to your heart:

> – How hard you are! Your brother pleads seventy excuses, yet you will not accept him. You are the one at fault, not your brother!

Even if it appears impossible to see things in a good light you ought not to get angry, if you can help it, though this may be asking too much. Al-Shafi'i (may God have mercy on him!) said:

> – If a man is provoked and does not get angry, he is an ass. If a man has cause for pleasure and is not pleased, he is a devil.

So don't be an ass or a devil! Give your heart cause to be pleased with yourself as your brother's deputy, and beware of being a devil if you fail to accept!

Al-Ahnaf said:

> – The duty of one's fellow is to bear three things: the wrong of anger, the wrong of over-familiarity, and the wrong of failings.

Another said:

> – I never malign anyone; for if he who maligns me is noble I am duty-bound to forgive him, while if he is base I do not let my honour be his target.

Then he coined this verse:

– The nobleman's fault I forgive, from
humility.

The abuse of the vile I ignore, from nobility.
Another poet said:
– Take from your friend what is pure, and let
alone the dross.

This life's too short for quarrelling, and
arguing the toss.

Whenever your brother apologises to you, accept
his excuse – be he lying or telling the truth. The Prophet
(may God bless him and give him Peace!) said:
– If a man's brother apologises to him and he
does not accept his excuse, he incurs a sin
like that of the tax-collector.[20]

He also said (God bless him and give him Peace!):
– The believer is quick to anger, quick to be
content.

He did not describe him as not getting angry.
Likewise God (Exalted is He!) said:
– . . . and who *contain* their wrath. (*Qur'ān
3.134*)[21]

He did not say, 'who *lose* their wrath.'

It does not normally happen that a man is wounded
physically without feeling pain, though he may endure
it patiently. But just as the pain from a wound is of the
nature of the physical body, so pain from the cause of
anger belongs to the nature of the heart. It cannot be
rooted out, though it can be controlled and repressed,
and its effects can be countered by seeking remedy,
revenge and retaliation. Moreover, it is possible to
refrain from acting under its influence.

The poet said:
– You cannot run with a brother and fail to

catch him in some disarray. What man is immaculate?

Abu Sulayman al-Darani said to Ahmad ibn Abi'l-Hawari:

> – If you take anyone as a brother in these times, do not remonstrate with him over what you disapprove of, for there is no guarantee that what you get in reply will not be worse than what you first complained of.

Said Ahmad:

> – I tested this out and found it to be so.

Someone said that patience with the pain caused by a brother is better than rebuking him in return, though rebuke is better than breaking off and breaking off is better than back-biting. If it should come to back-biting there should not be too much malice. God (Exalted is He!) said:

> – Perhaps God will create affection between you and those you have had as enemies. (*Qur'ān 60.7*)

The Prophet (God bless him and give him Peace!) said:

> – Go steady in loving your friend, for he may one day become your foe. Go steady in hating your foe, for he may become your friend one day.

'Umar (may God be pleased with him!) said:

> – Let not your love become attachment, nor your hate become destruction.

That is, by wishing your fellow's destruction at the cost of perishing yourself.

6

The sixth duty is to pray for your brother, during his
life and after his death, that he may have all he might
wish for himself, his family and his dependants.

You should pray for him as you pray for yourself,
making no distinction at all between you and him. For
in reality your prayer for him is a prayer for yourself.
The Prophet (God bless him and give him Peace!) said:

> – Whenever a man prays for his brother in
> secret, the angel says, 'And to you the same!'

In another version the words are:

> – . . . God (Exalted is He!) will say, 'I begin
> with you, My slave!'

According to the tradition:

> – A man's prayer on his brother's behalf will
> be answered, where that on his own account
> would go unanswered.

Also:

> – A man's prayer for his brother, in secret, is
> not rejected.

Abu'l-Darda' used to say:

> – I pray for seventy of my brothers during my
> prostration, naming them by their names.

Muhammad ibn Yusuf al-Isfahani used to say:

> – Where is the like of a virtuous brother? Your

family divide up your inheritance and enjoy what you leave behind, while he is alone in missing you, interested in what you have achieved and what has become of you, praying for you in the darkness of the night while you lie under layers of earth.

It seems that this virtuous brother follows in the steps of the angels, for according to the tradition:

> – When a man dies people ask, 'What did he leave behind?' But the angels say, 'What has he achieved?' They rejoice in his achievement, ask after him, and show compassion for him.

It is said that when a man, on hearing of his brother's death, asks for mercy on him and begs forgiveness for him, this is written in his favour as if he had attended his funeral and prayed over him.

It is related of God's Messenger (God bless him and give him Peace!) that he said:

> – The dead man in his grave is like one shipwrecked, completely dependent for everything. He waits for a prayer from a son or brother or relative.

Truly, lights like mountains enter the tombs of the dead from the prayer of the living. One of the early believers said:

> – Prayers for the dead are on the same footing as gifts for the living. The angel goes in to the dead with a tray of light, bearing a cloth of light, and says, 'This is a gift for you from your brother so-and-so, from your relative so-and-so.' And he delights in it just as a living man rejoices in a gift.

7

The seventh duty is loyalty and sincerity.

The meaning of loyalty is steadfastness in love and maintaining it to the death with your brother, and after his death with his children and his fellows. For love is for the sake of the Other Life. If it is severed before death the work is in vain and the effort wasted.

The Prophet (God bless him and give him Peace!) said:

> – Among the seven whom God keeps in His shadow are also two men who love each other for God's sake, constant whether together or apart.

Someone said:

> – A little loyalty after death is better than much during a lifetime.

Thus it is related that the Prophet (God bless him and give him Peace!) once gave a hearty welcome to an old woman who called upon him. When asked about it he said:

> – She used to come to us in the days of Khadija,[22] and honouring true friendship is part of religion.

Loyalty to the brother includes consideration towards all his fellows, relatives and dependants. To consider these is a greater duty in the heart of a fellow than to consider the brother himself, for his joy in care for those dependent on him is greater. Nothing proves the strength of compassion and love so much as when these carry over from the loved one to all his dependants. Even the dog at his gate should be distinguished in your heart from all other dogs! Whenever loyalty in sustaining love is broken Satan takes a malicious delight therein, for he does not envy two people who assist each other in good works as much as he envies two brothers, joined in brotherhood and love for God's sake. He exerts himself to spoil what is between them.

God (Exalted is He!) said:

> – Tell my servants to say what is kindlier. Surely, Satan sets them at variance. (*Qur'ān 17.53*)

And He said, in the story of Joseph:

> – . . . after Satan had sown discord between me and my brothers. (*Qur'ān 12.100*)

It is said that if a rupture falls between two who have become brothers in God, this can only be through a sin committed by one of them. Bishr used to say:

> – When the creature is remiss in obedience to God, God deprives him of someone intimate.

This is because brothers are a distraction from cares, and a help in religion. Ibn al-Mubarak said:

> – The sweetest thing of all is the company of brothers and reverting to sufficiency.

Lasting affection is that which is for the sake of God. That which has some other object passes away with the passing of that object.

One fruit of affection for God's sake is that envy cannot co-exist with it, whether in religion or in worldy affairs. How can one envy one's brother when all the benefit of what is his accrues to oneself? This is how God (Exalted is He!) describes those who love for His exalted sake:

> – They find no need in their breasts for what the others have been given, preferring them above themselves. (*Qur'ān 59.9*)

Finding need there would be envy.

Part of loyalty is not to let the relationship with the brother degenerate into humiliation. If one acquires importance, sees his authority expand and his dignity increase, and under these new conditions lords it over his brother, he is unworthy.

The poet said:

> – When the noble enjoy success they remember those who befriended them in their humble station.

One of the early believers counselled his son with these words:

> – My son, take no man for your fellow unless he draws near you when you need him and is not jealous of you when you can manage without him. When his station is exalted he should not lord it over you.

A wise man said:

> – If your brother acquires a position of authority, yet remains constant in one half of his affection, that is a great deal.

Al-Rabi' tells that al-Shafi'i (may God have mercy on him!) took for a brother a man of Baghdad. This brother became the governor of al-Saybayn, and changed

74

towards him. So al-Shafi'i wrote to him with these stanzas:

- Begone! For your affection from my heart
  is ever free.
  Though not yet by divorce irrevocable:
  Should you convert, there's been but one
  repudiation,
  And your affection still has two to go with me.
  Should you refuse, I'll match it with its like –
  Repudiations two, in menses two.
  When comes my third to you it will be
  absolute:
  Useless to you then the governorship of
  al-Saybayn![23]

Know that loyalty does not extend to concurring with a brother in what is contrary to the Truth in a matter of religion. Indeed loyalty then calls for opposition to him.

Al-Shafi'i (may God be pleased with him!) took as his brother Muhammad ibn Abd al-Hakam. He was his close and constant companion, and used to say:

- It is only he who keeps me in Egypt!

When Muhammad fell ill al-Shafi'i (may God have mercy on him!) visited him and said:

- The dear one fell sick, so I paid him a call.
  Then I too fell sick from concern over him.
  The dear one came to visit me,
  And I was cured by seeing him.

People expected, in view of the sincerity of their mutual affection, that al-Shafi'i would entrust to him the leadership of his circle after his death. Al-Shafi'i was asked during his death-sickness (may God have mercy on him!):

75

– At whose feet shall we sit when you are
gone, O Abu 'Abdullah?

Then Muhammad ibn 'Abd al-Hakam, who was by
his head, stood forward so that he could indicate him.
But al-Shafi'i said:

– Glory be to God! Can there by any doubt?
Abu Ya'qub al-Buwayti is the man!

Thus Muhammad's estimation was shattered, and
al-Shafi'i's followers turned to al-Buwayti. Although
Muhammad had learned the whole of his master's
teaching, nevertheless al-Buwayti was worthier and
closer to continence and piety. So al-Shafi'i was sincere
towards God and the Muslims. He forsook hypocrisy,
not preferring the pleasure of people to the pleasure of
God (Exalted is He!). On his death, Muhammad ibn
Abd al-Hakam turned away from his school and went
back to the school of his father, and to the study of the
books of Malik (may God have mercy on him!),
becoming one of the greatest of the followers of Malik
(may God have mercy on him!).

Al-Buwayti preferred abstinence and solitude. He
was not fond of company and sitting in the circle. He
occupied himself with worship and compiled *Kitāb
al-Umm*, which is now attributed to al-Rabi' ibn
Sulayman and goes under his name. Though it was
actually al-Buwayti who compiled it, he did not mention
himself in it, and did not ascribe it to himself. Al-Rabi'
added to it, edited it and published it.

The point is that part of the fulness of loyalty and
love is sincerity towards God. Al-Ahnaf said:

– Brotherhood is a subtle essence. If you do not
guard it, it is exposed to misfortunes. So guard
it by self-control, even to the point of apolo-

gising to one who has wronged you, and by contentment, so that you do not overrate your own virtues or your brother's failings.

One of the marks of truthfulness, sincerity and perfect loyalty is to be extremely wary of separation and instinctively shy of its causes. As it has been said:

– I found the blows of fate but trivial matters, except for the parting of friends.

Ibn ʿUyayna recited this stanza, and said:

– I have met up with folk from whom I had been apart for thirty years, never imagining that regret for them had left my heart.

Loyalty includes not listening to gossip about your friend, especially from one who first pretends to be dear to the friend so as to escape suspicion, but then speaks at random and conveys things about the friend which disturb the heart. This is one of the subtlest devices for stirring up strife. The affection of one unable to guard against it cannot be lasting at all.

Someone said to a wise man:

– I have come as suitor for your affection.

– I have set its dower at three things you must do.

– What are they?

– Do not listen to gossip about me. Do not oppose me in anything. Do not make me act rashly.

Loyalty includes not befriending your friend's enemy. Al-Shafiʿi (may God have mercy on him!) said:

– If your friend obeys your enemy, they share in enmity towards you.

77

8

The eighth duty is relief from discomfort and inconvenience.

You should not discomfort your brother with things that are awkward for him. Rather should you ease his heart of its cares and needs, and spare him having to assume any of your burdens. You should not ask him for help with money or influence. You should not discomfort him with having to be polite, to go into your situation and attend to your rights. No, the sole object of your love should be God (Exalted is He!), being blessed by your brother's prayer, enjoying his company, receiving assistance from him in your religion, drawing nigh to God (Exalted is He!) through attending to his rights and bearing his provision.

Someone said:

> – He who demands of his brothers what they do not demand, wrongs them. He who demands of them the same as they demand, wearies them. He who makes no demands is their benefactor.

One of the wise said:

> – He who sets himself with his brothers above his capacity sins, and they sin. He who sets himself at his capacity wearies, and wearies

them. He who sets himself below his capacity
is safe, and they are safe.

Complete relief means rolling up the carpet of
discomfort until he feels no more embarrassment from
you than from himself.

Al-Junayd said:

– If two become brothers for God's sake, and
one of them is uncomfortable or embarrassed
with his fellow, there must be a fault in one
of them.

'Ali (Peace upon him!) said:

– The worst of friends is one who discomforts
you and obliges you to be polite and to have
recourse to making apologies.

Al-Fudayl said:

– Discomfort is the cause of broken relations.
A man visits his brother, is made to feel
uncomfortable, and consequently breaks with
him.

'A'isha (may God be pleased with her!) said:

– The believer is brother to the believer. He
does not plunder him, nor does he embarrass
him.

Al-Junayd said:

– I have known the fellowship of four classes
of this party, thirty men to each class: Harith
al-Muhasibi and his class, Hasan al-Masuhi
and his class, Sari al-Saqati and his class, and
Ibn al-Karanbi and his class. If ever two
became brothers for the sake of God, and one
was discomforted or embarrassed by his
fellow, there was some fault in one of them.

Someone was asked:

– Whom shall we take for our fellow?

– One who will lift off you the heaviness of discomfort, and drop between you the load of formality.

Ja'far ibn Muhammad al-Sadiq (may God be pleased with him!) said:

– The heaviest of my brothers upon me is the one who discomforts me, and with whom I must observe formality. The lightest on my heart is he with whom I can be as I would be on my own.

One of the Sufis said:

– Do not be intimate with anyone unless piety will not increase his respect for you and sin will not diminish it. The merit or demerit should be yours, while his regard for you is the same.

He said this because in such a case there is freedom from discomfort and formality. Otherwise, nature would cause one to observe formality, knowing the risk of losing his esteem.

One of them said:

– Behave politely with sons of this world; with sons of the Other, wisely; with Those Who Know, as you wish.

Another said:

– Seek fellowship only with one who will repent for you if you sin, apologise for you if you do wrong, bear your burden for you and take care of his own.

The man who said this would make the way of brotherhood narrow for people. This is not how it should be. Rather should you seek the brotherhood of any intelligent, religious person, resolving to observe these conditions yourself, but not imposing such stipulations on the other. Then you will have many brothers, for you will be a brother for the sake of God. Otherwise, your brotherhood will be for your own convenience only.

A man said to al-Junayd:

> – Brothers are scarce in these times. Where am I to find a brother in God?

Al-Junayd made him repeat this thrice before replying:

> – If you want a brother to provide for *you* and to bear *your* burden, such – by my life – are few and far between. But if you want a brother in God whose burden you will carry and whose pain you will bear, then I have a troop I can introduce you to.

The man was silent.

Know that there are three kinds of people: a man from whose fellowship you can benefit; a man you can be of benefit to, and by whom you will not be hurt, though you cannot benefit from him; and a man whom you cannot benefit and by whom you will be hurt, namely the fool or man of evil character. The third type you should avoid. As for the second, do not shun him, for you will benefit in the Other World by his intercession and prayers, and by your reward for attending to him.

God (Exalted is He!) inspired unto Moses (Peace upon him!):

> – If you obey Me, how many are your brothers!

Meaning, if you console them, suffer them, and do not envy them.

Someone said:

> – I have kept the fellowship of people for fifty years without discord falling between us, for I have been with them as I would be on my own.

One who bears this mark has many brothers.

Relief and freedom from discomfort includes not objecting to supererogatory devotions. A group of Sufis used to engage in fellowship on condition of equality in four respects: If one of them ate all day his fellow would never say, 'Fast!'; if he fasted constantly he would never say, 'Break!'; if he slept all night through he would never say, 'Get up!'; and if he prayed all night through he would never say, 'Sleep!' Instead, he would follow suit, neither adding nor subtracting, because disparity moves the temperament to affectation and formality, without fail.

It has been said that if you drop your *kulfa* (formality), your *ulfa* (friendship) will last, and that if your burden is light you will have lasting affection.

One of the Companions of the Prophet said:

> – God has cursed those who cause discomfort.

And he (God bless him and give him Peace!) said:

> – I and the godly in my Community are free of formality.

Someone said:

> – If a man practises four things in his brother's house, then his society will be complete: if he eats with him, uses his toilet, prays and sleeps.

This was mentioned to one of the elders, who added:

> – A fifth remains, namely that he may bring his wife to his brother's house, and have

conjugal relations with her there. For the home is chosen for privacy in these five things, otherwise the mosques are more comfortable for the hearts of worshippers.

If he does these five things the brotherhood is complete, awkwardness is removed, and comfort is assured. The speech of the Arabs points to this, since their form of greeting is:

– *Marḥaban ahlan wa-sahlan*[24]

That is, 'You have a welcome with us, namely room in the heart and in the place; you have family with us, to enjoy their company without embarrassment from us; you have ease in all of this, that is, without anything you want being hard on us.'

Relief and lack of fuss is only complete when you consider yourself beneath your brothers and think highly of them, but poorly of yourself. When you consider them better than yourself you are actually better than they! Abu Mu'awiya al-Aswad said:

– All my brothers are better than I!
– How is that?
– Every one of them considers me more worthy than himself, and whoever rates me higher than himself is in fact better than I.

The Prophet (God bless him and give him Peace!) said:

– A man is on a par with the religion of his friend, and there is no good in the fellowship of one who does not regard you as highly as himself.

This is the least of the degrees; to look with the eye of equality. Perfection lies in seeing the greater merit in the brother.

Sufyan said:

> – If you are called 'O worst of men!' and you get angry, why, you are the worst of men.

That is, you must be convinced of that in yourself always.[25]

Several verses of poetry have been uttered on the subject of humility and looking up to one's brothers:

> – Be humble to those who thank you for it,
>   and do not think you a clown.
> Do not make friends with anyone who
>   on all his friends looks down.

Another said:

> – Many the friend I have met through a friend,
>   to find him closer than the old friend in the end.
> I meet many a mate, as my way I wend,
>   to find him the friend who will never pretend.

Whenever you see yourself superior to your brother, you belittle him, and this is blameworthy among Muslims in general. The Prophet (God bless him and give him Peace!) said:

> – The believer can do no worse than belittle his brother.

The completion of comfort and freedom from embarrassment includes consulting your brothers in all you plan, and in accepting their suggestions. He (Exalted is He!) said:

> – Consult them in the matter! (*Qur'ān 3.159*)

None of your secrets should be hidden from them. Consider the story of Ya'qub, the son of Ma'ruf's brother, who said:

84

– Aswad ibn Salim came to my uncle Ma'ruf, whose brother he had become, and said to him, 'Bishr ibn al-Harth wishes to take you for his brother, but he is shy of speaking to you about it face to face, so he sent me to ask you. If a bond of brotherhood is made between you and him, he will honour and respect it. Only he makes certain conditions: he does not want it to be publicised, nor for there to be any visiting and meeting between you, for he dislikes much meeting.' Ma'ruf said to this, 'As for me, if I take a brother I do not like to be parted from him night or day. I visit him at all times. I prefer him to myself under all circumstances.' Then he mentioned numerous Prophetic Traditions on the virtue of brotherhood and love for the sake of God, saying, 'One tradition has it that the Messenger of God (God bless him and give him Peace!) took 'Ali as his brother, making him his partner in knowledge and sharer in his body by giving him in marriage his most excellent and dearest daughter. This privilege he bestowed on him for the sake of his brotherhood. I now call you to witness that brotherhood is contracted between this man and me, and that I have bound myself in brotherhood to him for God's sake because of your message. As for the question of his visiting me; if he does not like that, well and good, but I shall visit him whenever I wish. Tell him that he will meet me in places where we shall meet. And tell him that he will not hide from me anything about himself, and that he will inform me of all his circumstances.' Ibn Salim reported this to him, and he agreed and was pleased about it.

Such then are the duties of fellowship. We have described them now in general, now in detail. But the matter is not complete unless they are taken to lie upon yourself and in your brothers' favour – not to lie upon them in yours – and unless you put yourself in the place of their servant. Therefore you must bind all your faculties to their service.

As for *sight*: by looking on them with affection, so that they will know it from you, and by looking on their good points and turning a blind eye to their faults. Do not distract your attention from them when they approach you, or as long as they are with you. It is related that the Prophet (God bless him and give him Peace!) used to give everyone who sat with him a share of his countenance, and that no-one sought his attention but thought him the most generous of men towards him. His sitting, his listening, his speaking, his kind enquiring and his attention were all for his companion. His company was a place of modesty, humility and confidence. Moreover, he (God bless him and give him Peace!) was of all men most given to smiling and laughing with his companions, and to marvelling at their tales. Following his example and doing him honour (on him be Peace!), his companions used to smile and laugh in his presence.

As for *hearing*: by listening to your brothers' words with pleasure and by confirming them, showing them to be well-received. Do not interrupt their speech wilfully or contentiously or intrusively or contradictingly. If a

86

distraction befalls you, apologise to them. Guard your hearing from what is distasteful to them.

As for the *tongue*: we have mentioned its duties already, there being much to say. One thing is not to raise your voice against them, and not to address them with things they do not understand.

As for the *hands*: by not withdrawing them from assisting your brothers in all that the hand can do.

As for the *feet*: by using them to walk behind like a follower, not striding out and not walking ahead unless they send you on in front, and not drawing close unless they summon you near. Stand for them when they approach you, and sit only when they are seated. Sit modestly when you sit.

When union is complete the burden of some of these duties is lifted (standing up, apologies and praise, for instance), for they are duties of fellowship and contain an element of remoteness and formality. When union is complete the carpet of formality is rolled up entirely, and you can behave with your brother as with yourself. For these manners of the Outer are only the title-page of the Inner and of Purity of Heart. When hearts are purified there is no need of formality to display their content.

He who looks to the fellowship of creatures will sometimes be crooked and sometimes straight. But he who looks to the Creator is bound to the Straight Path both inwardly and outwardly. His Inner is adorned by love of God and His creatures. His Outer is beautified by worship of God and service to His servants, for these

87

are the highest kinds of service to God, since there is no way to them except by good character. The slave can attain by the goodness of his character to the degree of the upright keeper of fasts – and beyond.

Postscript

In which we give a general account of the manners of social intercourse and of sitting in company with the various classes of men – culled from the words of the wise.

If you wish for a good social life, then be well-disposed toward your friend and your foe, without undue humility or fear, with dignity free of pride and modesty short of abasement. In all your dealings take the middle way, for both extremes of conduct are blameworthy.

Do not bear yourself haughtily or keep turning this way and that. Do not stand over assemblies, and when you sit down do not fidget. Beware of knitting your fingers, playing with your beard and ring, picking your teeth and poking your finger up your nose; of much spitting and nose-blowing and chasing flies from your face; of much stretching and yawning in people's faces – at the prayer and at other times.

Let your sitting be still, and your speech ordered and balanced. Attend to the good words of one who addresses you, without displaying excessive astonishment. Do not ask him to repeat himself.

Abstain from telling jokes and stories. Do not tell of your fondness for your children, your slave-girl, your poetry or prose, or other personal matters.

Do not affect the manners of women in adornment. Do not ape the extravagant manners of the slave. Beware of using too much kohl and excessive oil.

Do not press your needs. Do not encourage anyone to do wrong.

Do not let your wife and children, much less others, know the extent of your fortune. For if they consider it small you will seem mean in their eyes; if much, you will never succeed in satisfying them. Put them in fear without cruelty, and be gentle to them without weakness.

Do not joke with your slave-girl or your slave, for if you do you will lose their respect.

If you litigate, keep your dignity, be on guard against your ignorance, avoid undue haste and think of your proof. Do not make too many gestures with your hands, and do not turn around to those behind you. Do not squat on your knees. When your wrath has subsided then speak.

If a ruler approaches you, be with him as if on the tip of a spear. If he is familiar with you you have no guarantee that he will not turn against you. Be nice to him, as you would be to a little boy, and say things to please him, so long as it is nothing sinful. Do not let his kindness towards you induce you to enter his household among his wife and children and servants, even if he considers you entitled to do so. For the fall of one who comes between a king and his wife is a fall from which there is no rising, and an unspeakable slip.

Beware of the fair-weather friend, for he is the enemy of enemies.

Do not rank your wealth above your honour.

If you enter a session, the correct form is to give the salutation first, to yield to one who takes precedence, to sit where there is room and in the humblest place, to greet with 'Salaam' those next to where you sit. Do not sit in the path.

Once seated, the correct form is to lower the eyes, to help the wronged, to support the distressed, to aid the weak, to direct the lost, to return the greeting, to give to the beggar, to enjoin good and forbid evil, to find a place to spit and not to spit towards the *qibla*[26] nor to the right, but only to the left or under the left foot.

Do not sit in the company of kings, but if you do, the manner is to abandon slander and avoid untruth, to guard the secret, to have few wants, to polish your words and converse in fully-inflected Arabic, to discourse in the style of kings, to show little frivolity and much caution – even if affection is shown to you. Do not belch in their presence, and do not pick your teeth after eating.

It is the king's duty to suffer everything except the divulging of secrets, *lèse majesté* and sacrilege.

Do not sit in company with the mob, but if you do, the correct behaviour is to avoid engaging them in conversation, to pay little heed to their false-alarms, to ignore the bad language current among them, and to confine intercourse with them to the necessary minimum.

Beware of jesting with the intelligent or the unintelligent, for the intelligent will feel rancour towards you, while the profligate will be emboldened against you. Jesting punctures respect and causes loss of face. It leads to rancour and takes away the sweetness of affection. It mars the understanding of the perceptive and emboldens the profligate. It lowers one's standing with the wise and is disliked by the godfearing. It is death to the heart, and sets one apart from the Lord

91

(Exalted is He!). It earns neglect and an inheritance of abasement. Hearts are harmed by it and minds are killed by it. It multiplies faults and makes sins apparent. It has been said:

> – There is no jesting but from folly or insolence.

One who is afflicted in a sitting by jesting or babble should remember God when he gets up. The Prophet (God bless him and give him Peace!) said:

> – He who sits in a session and babbles a lot should say before he rises from that sitting, 'Glory to Thee, our God! With Thy praise I testify that there is no deity save Thee! I ask Thy forgiveness and I repent to Thee!'

Surely He will forgive him for what happened in that session of his.

Translator's Notes

1. There are arguments in favour of the spelling 'al-Ghaz-zali'. In fact controversy over the correct form of the name constitutes a minor branch of Oriental scholarship. To medieval Europe he was known as 'Algazel'.

2. The word 'Assassin' probably derives from the Arabic *hashshāshīn*, meaning 'hashish-takers'.

3. Al-Azhar was to become – and remains to this day – the very citadel of orthodox Islamic teaching. Fatimid power in Egypt was finally broken in 1171 by the famous Saladin.

4. As indicated by the 'al-Shafi'i' in his name, al-Ghazali's legal studies followed the teachings of the great jurist al-Shafi'i, founder of one of the four main schools of Islamic jurisprudence.

5. The Arabic title may also be translated as 'The Inconsistency of the Philosophers'.

6. A. L. Tibawi, *Islamic Education*, London, 1972, p. 31.

7. W. Montgomery Watt, *Islamic Philosophy and Theology*, Edinburgh, 1962, p. 114. The reader who wishes to know more about al-Ghazali is recommended to turn to this and other works by Professor Montgomery Watt namely, *The Faith and Practice of al-Ghazali*, London, 1951; *Muslim Intellectual: the Struggle and Achievement of al-Ghazali*, Edinburgh, 1963. These will also provide references to further reading on the subject.

8. Parts of the *Ihyā'* have been translated into European

languages, but the present translator has not been able to trace any other version, in a European tongue, of the section 'On the Duties of Brotherhood' although there is a précis of it in G. H. Bousquet's analysis in French of the whole *Iḥyā'*.

9. Al-Ghazali has treated elsewhere on the subject of the proper conduct of marriage.

10. 'faithful witness to the truth.'

11. The *ṣalāt* is the ritual prayer performed by Muslims at five prescribed times during the day – dawn, midday, afternoon, sunset and evening.

12. 'There is no fault . . . in your eating from your houses, or your fathers' houses, or your mothers' houses, or your brothers' houses, or your sisters' houses, or the houses of your uncles and aunts, paternal and maternal, *or of your friend, or to which you have the keys.*'

13. 'They only answer who hear. *As for the dead, God will raise them up.*'

14. *Takbīr* is the exclamation, *Allāhu akbar!*, meaning 'God is Most Great!' Arabic derives its vocabulary from roots of three consonants, so from the k-b-r of *akbar*, for instance, it forms a verb *kabbara*, meaning, 'he exclaimed "God is Most Great!" ', and a noun *takbīr*, meaning 'the utterance of the exclamation "God is Most Great!" '. This is an indication of the pregnant character of much Arabic writing, and of the allusive capacities of the language.

15. 'Muhammad is the Messenger of God, and those who are with him are hard against the unbelievers, *full of mercy one to another.*'

16. *Al-amru bi'l-ma 'rūfi wa-'l-nahyu 'ani 'l-munkar*, meaning

'to promote good and prevent evil', is an overriding duty for the Muslim.

17. This is a reference to the pagan Arab custom of disposing of unwanted female offspring.

18. 'Muslim' means one characterised by *Islam* – literally 'submission (to the Will of God)'. Through 'right belief' or 'true faith' – *Iman* – he may become a 'Mu'min'. The term *Iman* is often confused, in Western writings of a general nature, with the word *Imam*, meaning 'prayer-leader'.

19. *Ḥa' Mim*: two letters of the Arabic alphabet. Several chapters of the Qur'an begin with such letters. They remain a mystery, though many interpretations have been suggested.

20. One who collects duties not authorised in Sacred Law.

21. Part of a description of those for whom Paradise is prepared.

22. The Prophet Muhammad's first wife, and the first person to believe in his mission.

23. Al-Shafi'i's metaphor in this poem is the procedure of divorce by triple repudiation. Only after the third step is immediate reconciliation impossible.

24. 'Welcome, family, and ease!'

25. Al-Ghazali notes that he will discuss the subject more fully in the book of Pride and Vanity.

26. *Qibla* – the direction of Mecca towards which all Muslims pray.